Jean Ingelow

Songs of Seven

Jean Ingelow

Songs of Seven

ISBN/EAN: 9783744776035

Printed in Europe, USA, Canada, Australia, Japan

Cover: Foto ©Thomas Meinert / pixelio.de

More available books at **www.hansebooks.com**

BY

JEAN INGELOW.

Illustrated.

BOSTON:

ROBERTS BROTHERS.

1885.

JOHN WILSON & SON. UNIVERSITY PRESS. CAMBRIDGE.

The full-page illustrations are designed by Miss C. A. NORTHAM and J. FRANCIS MURPHY; the titlepage, and those in the text, by EDMUND H. GARRETT. The book is prepared and the illustrations engraved by GEO. T. ANDREW.

CONTENTS

EXULTATION.

"I am seven times one to-day."

SONGS OF SEVEN.

Seven times One.

EXULTATION.

THERE'S no dew left on the daisies and clover
 There's no rain left in heaven;
I've said my " seven times " over and over,
 Seven times one are seven.

I am old, so old, I can write a letter;
 My birthday lessons are done;
The lambs play always, they know no better;
 They are only one times one.

O moon! in the night I have seen you sailing
  And shining so round and low;
You were bright! ah bright! but your light is
    failing:
  You are nothing now but a bow

You moon, have you done something wrong in
    heaven
  That God has hidden your face?
I hope if you have you will soon be forgiven,
  And shine again in your place.

O velvet bee, you're a dusty fellow,
  You've powdered your legs with gold!
O brave marsh marybuds, rich and yellow,
  Give me your money to hold!

O columbine, open your folded wrapper,
  Where two twin turtle-doves dwell !
O cuckoopint, toll me the purple clapper
  That hangs in your clear green bell.

And show me your nest with the young
        ones in it ;
  I will not steal them away;
I am old ! you may trust me, linnet, linnet :
  I am seven times one to-day.

Seven times Two.

ROMANCE.

Y OU bells in the steeple, ring, ring out your
changes,
How many soever they be,
And let the brown meadow-lark's note as he
ranges
Come over, come over to me.

Yet bird's clearest carol by fall or by swelling
No magical sense conveys,
And bells have forgotten their old art of telling
The fortune of future days.

ROMANCE.

"I wait for my story — the birds cannot sing it."

"Turn again, turn again," once they rang cheerily,
　While a boy listened alone;
Made his heart yearn again, musing so wearily
　All by himself on a stone.

Poor bells! I forgive you; your good days are over,
　And mine, they are yet to be;
No listening, no longing, shall aught, aught discover:
　You leave the story to me.

The foxglove shoots out of the green matted heather,
　Preparing her hoods of snow;
She was idle, and slept till the sunshiny weather:
　O, children take long to grow.

I wish, and I wish that the spring would go faster,
  Nor long summer bide so late;
And I could grow on like the foxglove and aster,
  For some things are ill to wait.

I wait for the day when dear hearts shall discover,
  While dear hands are laid on my head;
" The child is a woman, the book may close over,
  For all the lessons are said."

I wait for my story — the birds cannot sing it,
  Not one, as he sits on the tree;
The bells cannot ring it, but long years, O bring it
  Such as I wish it to be.

LOVE.

"Dark, dark was the garden, I saw not the gate."

Seven times Three.

LOVE.

I LEANED out of window, I smelt the white
    clover,
  Dark, dark was the garden, I saw not the gate;
"Now, if there be footsteps, he comes, my one
    lover —
  Hush, nightingale, hush! O, sweet nightingale,
    wait
        Till I listen and hear
        If a step draweth near,
        For my love he is late!

" The skies in the darkness stoop nearer and nearer,
A cluster of stars hangs like fruit in the tree,
The fall of the water comes sweeter, comes clearer :
To what art thou listening, and what dost thou see?
Let the star-clusters glow,
Let the sweet waters flow,
And cross quickly to me.

" You night-moths that hover where honey brims
over
From sycamore blossoms, or settle or sleep ;
You glow-worms, shine out, and the pathway dis-
cover
To him that comes darkling along the rough steep.
Ah, my sailor, make haste,
For the time runs to waste,
And my love lieth deep —

" Too deep for swift telling; and yet, my one lover
   I've conned thee an answer, it waits thee to-night."
By the sycamore passed he, and through the white
    clover,
   Then all the sweet speech I had fashioned took
    flight;
        But I'll love him more, more
        Than e'er wife loved before,
        Be the days dark or bright.

Seven times Four.

MATERNITY.

HEIGH-HO! daisies and buttercups,
    Fair yellow daffodils, stately and tall!
When the wind wakes how they rock in the grasses,
    And dance with the cuckoo-buds slender and
        small!
Here's two bonny boys, and here's mother's own
        lasses,
        Eager to gather them all.

MATERNITY.

"Heigh-ho! daisies and buttercups!
Mother shall thread them a daisy chain."

Heigh-ho! daisies and buttercups!
Mother shall thread them a daisy chain;
Sing them a song of the pretty hedge-sparrow,
That loved her brown little ones, loved them
full fain;
Sing, " Heart, thou art wide though the house be
but narrow," —
Sing once, and sing it again.

Heigh-ho! daisies and buttercups,
Sweet wagging cowslips, they bend and they bow;
A ship sails afar over warm ocean waters,
And haply one musing doth stand at her prow.
O bonny brown sons, and O sweet little daughters,
Maybe he thinks on you now!

Heigh-ho! daisies and buttercups,
    Fair yellow daffodils, stately and tall —
A sunshiny world full of laughter and leisure,
    And fresh hearts unconscious of sorrow and thrall!
Send down on their pleasure smiles passing its meas-
        ure,
        God that is over us all!

WIDOWHOOD.

"I lift mine eyes, and what to see
But a world happy and fair!"

Seven times Five.

WIDOWHOOD.

I SLEEP and rest, my heart makes
    moan
  Before I am well awake:
"Let me bleed! O let me alone,
  Since I must not break!"

For children wake, though fathers
    sleep
  With a stone at foot and at head:
O sleepless God, for ever keep,
  Keep both living and dead!

I lift mine eyes, and what to see
   But a world happy and fair!
I have not wished it to mourn with
      me,—
   Comfort is not there.

O what anear but golden brooms,
   And a waste of reedy rills!
O what afar but the fine glooms
   On the rare blue hills!

   I shall not die, but live forlore—
     How bitter it is to part!
   O to meet thee, my love, once more!
     O my heart, my heart!

No more to hear, no more to see!
  O that an echo might wake
And waft one note of thy psalm to me
  Ere my heart strings break !

        I should know it how faint soe'er,
          And with angel-voices blent ;
        O once to feel thy spirit anear,
          I could be content.

Or once between the gates of gold,
  While an entering angel trod,
But once — thee sitting to behold
  On the hills of God !

Seven times Six.

GIVING IN MARRIAGE.

TO bear, to nurse, to rear,
　　To watch, and then to lose:
To see my bright ones disappear,
　　Drawn up like morning dews—
To bear, to nurse, to rear,
　　To watch, and then to lose:
This have I done when God drew
　　　near
　　Among his own to choose.

GIVING IN MARRIAGE.

"Thy mother's tenderest words are said,
Thy face no more she views."

To hear, to heed, to wed,
  And with thy lord depart
In tears that he, as soon as shed,
  Will let no longer smart. —
To hear, to heed, to wed,
  This while thou didst I smiled,
For now it was not God who said,
  "Mother, give ME thy child."

O fond, O fool, and blind,
  To God I gave with tears;
But when a man like grace would find,
  My soul put by her fears.
O fond, O fool, and blind,
  God guards in happier spheres;
That man will guard where he did bind
  Is hope for unknown years.

To hear, to heed, to wed,
　　Fair lot that maidens choose,
Thy mother's tenderest words are said,
　　Thy face no more she views;
Thy mother's lot, my dear,
　　She doth in naught accuse;
Her lot to bear, to nurse, to rear,
　　To love — and then to lose.

LONGING FOR HOME.

"Can I call that home where I anchor yet,
Though my good man has sailed?"

Seven times Seven.

LONGING FOR HOME.

A SONG of a boat : —
   There was once a boat on a billow :
Lightly she rocked to her port remote,
   And the foam was white in her wake like snow,
And her frail mast bowed when the breeze would
      blow,
   And bent like a wand of willow.

I shaded mine eyes one day when a boat
    Went curtseying over the billow,
I marked her course till a dancing mote
She faded out on the moonlit foam,
And I stayed behind in the dear loved home;
    And my thoughts all day were about the boat,
    And my dreams upon the pillow.

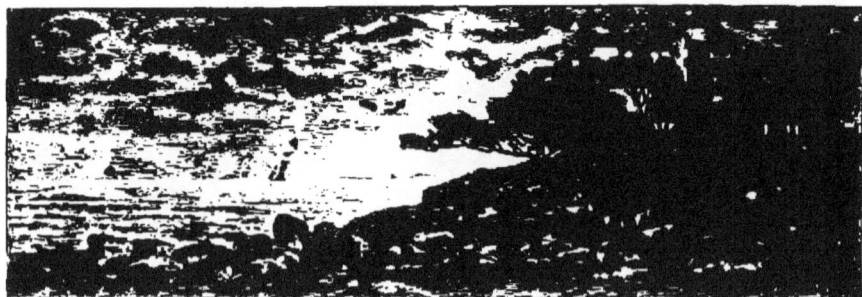

I pray you hear my song of a boat,
    For it is but short: —
My boat, you shall find none fairer afloat,
    In river or port.
Long I looked out for the lad she bore,
    On the open desolate sea,
And I think he sailed to the heavenly shore,
    For he came not back to me —
            Ah me!

A song of a nest : —
There was once a nest in a hollow :
Down in the mosses and knot-grass
    pressed,
Soft and warm, and full to the brim.
Vetches leaned over it purple and dim,
    With buttercup buds to follow.

I pray you hear my song of a nest,
    For it is not long : —
You shall never light, in a summer quest
    The bushes among —
Shall never light on a prouder sitter,
    A fairer nestful, nor ever know
A softer sound than their tender twitter,
    That wind-like did come and go.

I had a nestful once of my own,
    Ah happy, happy I!
Right dearly I loved them: but when they
        were grown
    They spread out their wings to fly.
O, one after one they flew away
    Far up to the heavenly blue,
To the better country, the upper day,
    And — I wish I was going too.

I pray you, what is the nest to me,
    My empty nest?
And what is the shore where I stood to see
    My boat sail down to the west?
Can I call that home where I anchor yet,
    Though my good man has sailed?

Can I call that home where my nest was set,
　　Now all its hope hath failed?
Nay, but the port where my sailor went,
　　And the land where my nestlings be, —
There is the home where my thoughts are sent,
　　The only home for me —
　　　　　Ah me!

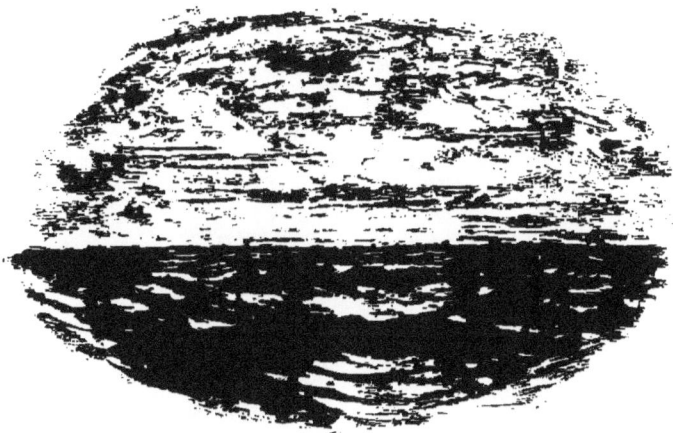

www.ingramcontent.com/pod-product-compliance
Lightning Source LLC
Chambersburg PA
CBHW021443090426
42739CB00009B/1625